Understanding the System of White Patriarchy:

Think Like the White Man

Authored by Julius M. Long

Understanding the System of White Patriarchy:
Think Like the White Man
Copyright © 2018 by Julius M. Long

ISBN: 978-0-692-10958-8

Table of Contents

Foreword

It's not often that a [black] father is asked to write a foreword to his son's book. Therefore, I am humbled that my son Julius Martin Long, granted me this honorable task.

"Understanding the System of White Patriarchy: Think Like the White Man," is a confrontational dialogue that challenges and encourages African Americans that are seeking change; to accomplish it through self-sufficiency and to approach the challenges of life with an understanding of the "White Man's Mentality," more specifically White Patriarchy.

As a child growing up, Julius was an independent thinker that challenged societal "norms" intellectually and believed that there was always an alternative method to achieve any outcome. He believed that the road to accomplishing the same outcomes as whites was more difficult for people of color.

He understood at an early age, that it's not what you know in life, but who you know that helps you achieve success. He also realized that "good fortune" manifests when preparation meets opportunity. He has prepared himself educationally by obtaining his B.S. degree in Economics from Florida Agricultural and Mechanical University (FAMU).

During my years as an entrepreneur, community activist, and former elected city and county official for over three decades, Julius has observed and learned how to network with movers and shakers and how to press the flesh to help himself and others to become successful. He understands that two engines drive our society, economics and politics. He is involved in both.

Julius is an entrepreneur that believes that if you're going to make it in life, you need to be willing to take risks and not be afraid to fail. To date, his businesses J. Long Productions, LLC, and Music Express United Records, located in Gainesville, Florida, has its tentacles in several directions. He's an accomplished recording artist, writer, producer, concert promoter, booking agent, artist manager and now… an intriguing author.

He believes in giving back to his community. He recently established "Lil' Afrika," a resource center for disadvantaged youth. His commitment to political involvement led him to launch DAB to Vote, a voting-registration campaign that educates millennial voters regarding political candidates and community issues.

Julius Long has a keen understanding of the "White Man" [America's patriarchal system], especially as it relates to using "their" tools to overcome challenges and move ahead! His new book, "Understanding the System of White Patriarchy: Think Like the White Man", is provocative, engaging, and a "must-read" for anyone who has questioned America's patriarchal system.

Honorable Rodney J. Long
Former Mayor-Commissioner City of Gainesville, Florida
Former Alachua County Commissioner of Gainesville/
Alachua County, Florida
Former President of Florida Association of Counties (FAC)
Email: rodneyjlong@gmail.com

Introduction

DON'T JUDGE THIS BOOK BY IT'S COVER!

To understand this book, there is *one* requirement; put aside your egos, pessimism, and biased thoughts.

This research was prompted by one question. *What does the conservative white man think regarding the black man?* So, I pondered, could his thoughts be my thoughts even if he didn't understand me? If I approached life the way *he* did, would I or could I, be where *he* is in life? At this point, I know some of my readers are thinking, "How and why, would a young black man want to think like a white man?" The answer to this question provokes an understanding of the white patriarchal system everyone lives in *today*.

There are many black men that are slothful, complacent, and too stubborn to think beyond their personal ideologies/philosophies. It is imperative to understand white patriarchy, in order to grasp the rationale of daily interactions and the concept of success within our white-washed society. We MUST acquire, analyze, and apply *this* knowledge to various situations in our lives.

More than anything else, we must realize that we live in a Eurocentric society and the things that transpire [daily], are not geared toward the cultural lifestyle of the black male. Every system we encounter is monopolized by the thought process of a white male (education, government, religion, the media, and social media). These systems structure, control, and manipulate everything that happens within our society.

Fortunately, this simplistic burst of enlightenment will give you a sense of accomplishment and completion. Allow this book to ignite and revitalize your mind. You have nothing to lose, knowledge will always be the most powerful asset we possess.

Gratitude & Dedication

I give honor to God and the ascended masters in their respective places. I thank my parents (Mr. & Mrs. Rodney J. Long) for a sound upbringing and their willing sacrifices to provide me with opportunities to *be* successful in today's society. I pay homage to my family and ancestors for paving the path for a better future. My adversities, failures, and successes allowed me to think and perceive life the way I do, and for this I am grateful! I thank everyone that offered me encouragement as well as criticism, all of *it* has propelled me to this pivotal point in my life. I am truly thankful.

I dedicate this book to people who attained an understanding of the way life works in America. This book is for the dreamers who manifested their dreams as realities. Moreover, this literary work is for the *first-time* readers, who have now embarked on a journey of knowledge and mind-renewal. Thank you for joining *this movement*

Chapter 1: The Establishment of White Privilege

When I decided to author this book, I knew this chapter would be combatively intriguing. Consequently, I mentally prepared myself for the inevitable backlash. For any white person that has had the audacity to *claim* they have not benefited from their "whiteness," this is a factual lie (oxymoronic, yes, it is).

Primarily, we must understand the meaning of "white privilege." According to Cambridge English Dictionary, white privilege is the advantage within a society that non-white citizens do not have under the same social, political, or economic circumstances. Academic perspectives such as Critical Race Theory and Whiteness Studies use the concept of "white privilege" to analyze how racism and racialized societies affect the lives of white and/or white-skinned people.

I asked a young black male the following question, "What does white privilege mean to you?" He replied, "White privilege is something I do not have as a *black* man." I also asked a young black female this same question, and she retorted, "It keeps blacks from pursuing *certain* opportunities because we lack white privilege." In our American society, *all* White people benefit from *white privilege*. This benefit gives a sense of pre-established prestige where even poor white people possess *it*.

Since the beginning of the new world discovery, every provision, decision, (judicial and criminal), and economic security has been in favor of white men (and women). Black slaves labored to build this country and white people reaped all the benefits, (agriculturally, financially, educationally, and technologically). Historically, white privilege was a blatant inclusion of subjugation that read, "White only" from bathrooms to banks.

White privilege constructed America's prison systems, thus the rate of incarceration for nonviolent crimes for blacks compared to whites is shockingly disproportionate. Black men are incarcerated in state prisons at a rate five-times higher than whites; while the use of drugs and the rate of committed crimes between these races are the same.

Some may still think white privilege is nothing more than utter malarkey. I dare to ask *that* person this one simple question: "Would *you* like to trade places with *me*?" In order to understand [my] life or the life of any African American, one must spend at least half of their life as one. White privilege is alive, breathing, and it is quite unapologetic.

Would you want to endure the pain and relentless hardship [my] race has suffered in the United States: the slavery, educational injustices, income disparities, racial inequality, and *your* oblivious white privilege? If your answer to this question is "no," then you'll answer "yes" to the fact that racism still exists, and you have inadvertently acknowledged there is an unjust bias in our country's systematic structure. My next question now is, are you willing to *think* for change?

Is it possible, that white people don't live in the same world that Blacks live in?

Of course, they don't. They don't have the same goals or fears. They don't like what Blacks like. The influence of white privilege shaped the mentality of whites. Thus, because their perception of society is different, so is *their* world. Perception is reality.

We are all Americans correct?

What race comes to your mind when you hear the term "American?" I can fairly assume most people imagined a white male that looks as if he just walked out of Abercrombie & Fitch. I imagined a white man too, but he was a systematic serial killer. The system of institutionalized laws that has kept people that look like me suppressed mentally, educationally,

4

socially, and financially. Consequently, black men (and women) across this world have witnessed and experienced the systemic killing of their hopes and dreams, simply because they did not fully understand *how* to combat white privilege.

Chapter 2: Sense of Entitlement

Understanding white privilege, is the key to combating it. We cannot fight or overcome the things we fail to understand. This is the "sixth-sense" that all black men (and women) have. If we don't understand anything else, we fully comprehend the injustices and blatant disregard of our humanness at the hands of white patriarchy. Our "sixth-sense" can detect white privilege without seeing it or hearing it – because we feel and perceive it *first*.

It is felt, when we are apprehended for driving while black, and told we were stopped for an improper turn at a four-way stop. It is felt, when have no criminal history, twice the work experience, and two degrees, but the job we applied for is given to a "white male" because he fits the "look" of the company. It is felt, when we witness or hear about another innocent life killed or assaulted at the hands of "justified" police officers, and the acquittal is celebrated by

6

white America. It is felt. White privilege – the sense of entitlement for whites (especially men).

Do Whites understand why we (blacks) "stand-up" for our people?

Adequate resources and opportunities are assets most white people have always had, it is not something they had to win (or fight for). Thus their sense of entitlement, resides in a place of expectation because they have not experienced anything contrary to their comfortable realities. However, black people have been fighting against this "sense of entitlement" for hundreds of years. Most whites are aware of this concept and will never fully understand it. People cannot identify with the things they do not understand; if they haven't experienced it, *it* is that much more difficult to conceptualize *it*. If you have never experienced a situation how can you have any sympathy or concern regarding that situation?

Most whites do not understand our struggle because they do not know our pain. They cannot understand our rage because our life is not their stage. They will not give us a hand-up or hand-out because they reserve it for their friends and kin. So, when I asked if they understood why we stand-up for ours, what I really meant to say is... Do they understand why we sometimes feel like we lack *real* power?

I wonder if we were to switch places in America, would we be better off individually?

Some of my peers and I have frequently discussed the hierarchy of race in America. We all know (or should know) that race is socially constructed entity. We were all born to one race - the human race, and white patriarchy established the idea of race based on physical attributes and their personal preferences. Consequently, the mandate of racially constructed society benefited the creators expectantly (no surprise).

Therefore, if the primary races "switched" places in America, the outcome would not change. Power and preference always established a "fixed" and biased foundation. So, no one would be better off, and our society would experience the same turmoil and the battle for justice and equality would be a constant fight just as it is now.

In order to withstand white patriarchy (WP), black men (BM) [and women] must understand white patriarchy.

WP: The thought process of a black man differs greatly from a white man's perspective. Does the black man understand where he comes from? I don't know I'm not him. I know blacks had to come from Africa. It's pretty hot, but you guys had a beautiful culture and a very unique understanding of the universe. The architecture and buildings all over the world are amazingly mind-blowing. I wanted to incorporate some of those ideas in my homeland.

BM: We were forced into slavery and bondage, shackled and chained. We were transported to the Americas on ships (we endured rape, sodomy, abuse, eradication of our identity, and unspeakable humiliation). Eventually, we were granted complete humanity and were emancipated from slavery. We had courageous leaders like Harriet Tubman, Frederick Douglas, Sojourner Truth, Nat Turner, Rosa Parks, Martin Luther King, Malcolm X., Muhammad Ali, George Washington Carver, Benjamin Banneker, Jackie Robinson and many more. We learn about these great people in the *long* month of February only, because American history is taught and celebrated throughout the year. Quite frequently I wonder, what does it mean to be an American while being black?

White patriarchy sounds like "Servants can pay their debt in labor for a great opportunity in the New World." White patriarchy believes, "There is no way those uncivilized African people built the pyramids, had thriving civilizations, and were far more advanced mathematically and scientifically than any other nation!" White patriarchy has taught, "The brain of a black person is significantly smaller than any other race, thus their intellectual capabilities are significantly less than all other races."

Chapter 3: The Appearance of Success & Wealth

The concept of success and wealth within the black community has primarily been attributed to sports and entertainment. Unfortunately, several black athletes and entertainers have not maintained their perceived level of wealth or success. Too often the idea of success and wealth is a correlation between material possessions and the appearance of "being rich." Success is much more than the attainment of a nice home, luxury vehicles, and a six-figure income; and wealth is much more than a person's individual net worth.

There are too many black men that would rather look rich than attain residual wealth. Consequently, the idea of success is attached to materialism and not the establishment of innovative ideas. The black community must be and become innovative business owners! Ownership and innovation work together.

Conversely, oppression is a part of tradition and white patriarchy has attempted to oppress the greatness of black men (and women) everywhere! We must be thinkers to remain two steps ahead of the game. It's the refocusing we lack. We are not updating our culture and community.

Who have we been training for the last 20 years to continue the legacy? Who is being molded?

We are closing the doors on our own people and short stopping our kids' future. We don't know our history. This fact affects our ability to embrace who we truly are, our identity is directly connected to our history. We need to be bold. What are we doing? Do we have *what it takes?*

I recently asked a black sixteen-year-old male the following question: "From your perspective, how do white men perceive you?" He replied, "Their goal is to kill us!" He explained, "Donald Trump is the epitome of white privilege, and I have observed and experienced the residual effects of white privilege since I was in elementary school." "I see fear

13

and failure constantly, and it seems impossible to be hopeful or slightly optimistic." Immediately I asked myself, what if everything the sixteen-year old saw was positive and joyful. Would this provoke a different response?

If Black men and boys are exposed to different ideas and realities, then their mentalities are destined to change, and it forces them to think beyond the typical notions of success and wealth. However, a large proportion of black men have never been taught or exposed to the intricate working of the financial market (banking, credit, investments, and residual income).

Thus, this is an educational dilemma as well as support issue. Who is raising the current generation? Who are their role models? Why are they seemingly so lost? The black community needs more than another rapper or athlete, because their influence is clearly more of a liability than it is an asset.

Chapter 4: Value and Worth

In today's business world, we have lost our values. We don't fully understand our worth or the value in refusing to "sell-out." We have the tendency to build up our businesses only to sell them to the highest bidder. Most of the time, blacks are not the highest bidder. Our Caucasian counterparts understand the value of generational wealth. They build their establishments and legacies only to pass them down to their children, and their children improve, increase, and maintain that wealth.

Why do we [the black community] have so many people doing the same things?

Our possibilities are limitless, if we can tap into the power of raising each other up instead tearing each other down, our communities will thrive in all aspects.

Black people are some of the most intelligent, innovative, forward-thinkers this world has known. Without the contributions of blacks, America would not be the greatest nation. Therefore, our communities should be a direct reflection of the greatness that was stripped from us, and forcefully proclaimed as the innovative greatness of white men.

Black men (and women) can own more than food trucks, bootleg cd/dvd collections, and knock-off designer bags sold from the trunks of their cars. These depictions are glorified in the media, and sadly accepted as the reality of black communities worldwide. Fortunately, I have been exposed to more.

I know and work with black lawyers, government officials, police officers, teachers, editors, investors, and financial experts. It is the influence of these people that have helped shaped my reality, my mentality, and caused me to have an aversion towards mediocrity!

Money Talks black people, let's get our money right!

It is an economic fact that black consumers spend most of their income on material things and save the least amount of their income than any other race in America. Many of us lack the ability to successfully manage our finances. The misappropriation of personal funds has a direct correlation between the lack of wealth among blacks in the financial world. It's easy for us to make money, but our management skills are quite lackadaisical.

Understanding the difference between gross and net pay is vital to economic competence. In economics, maximizing profits or **profit maximization** is the short run or long run process by which a business determines the price and output level that returns the greatest profit. In order for blacks to reach their full potential, we cannot be afraid to step out the norm to grow your business. We must be open to new innovative ways to spend less money and make more.

When I completed my bachelor's Degree in Economics at Florida A&M University, I found it relatively simple once I understood the basics. I have been applying these principles to my life since I acquired this skill-set. Even in our school system today, economics is a subject most students shy away from. Every choice that we make is an economical decision. The choice one makes to stay home and cook versus spending twenty dollars on takeout food. The decision to buy water by the cases from the store to get a cheaper price in bulk instead of paying more for a smaller quantity.

Simplistic decisions to pay attention to how we spend our money will improve the financial situation of black people everywhere. Convenience is not the litmus test of a wise decision! However, all wise decisions are coupled with actions that are *usually* inconvenient or difficult.

Chapter 5: Stock Market vs. Street Market

Economic principles are applied in life as well as in the streets. Any individual that understands the concept of the drug industry will make an awesome economist. My former street endeavors allowed me to thoroughly understand and enjoy economics [*I realized selling nickel bags, dimes, quarter ounces were all with micro manageable quantities*].

These swings (sells), were managed by my homeboy (friend). This *minor* money was not my concern. I wanted to deal with the real money. The real money resided in wholesales. If you wanted to purchase pounds in large quantities, that's macroeconomics. Once I understood that buying in bulk would get me a cheaper price from "The connect," I realized, I could stretch my money (make more) off the same amount of product which is essentially maximizing profit.

I am not advocating for the illegal practice of street pharmacy to get a degree (selling drugs), however, I am pointing out that we must understand everything is a business in this white patriarchal society. Once we identify this principle, we can look at the financial market differently. Billions of dollars are generated annually in this black-market economy. Think about it. To understand finding a "plug" (connections, resources) to get your product at its minimum cost for the best quality, is outsourcing in its most simplistic manner, and sometimes involves international trade as well.

Some people even go to the extent of learning Spanish to find a plug. What if we [black men] applied this knowledge and energy into something positive, or even treated all businesses like "the white man?" Think about if we stop buying rims, cars, clothes, jewelry, and throwing money at the club and start investing our finances in more real estate, agriculture, education and college funds for our children, or reinvesting in the existing businesses, we would be the black Rockefellers, Kennedys, or the Walton's.

What if we put this same energy into the stock market and educated ourselves regarding financial investments and financial freedom? Not to mention financial aid disbursements and collegiate scholarships are another reason to attend college.

Definition of 'Black Economy,' The segment of a country's economic activity that is derived from sources that fall outside of the country's rules and regulations regarding commerce. The activities can be either legal or illegal depending on what goods and/or services are involved.

After taking another statistical analysis of the ROI (Return on Investment) or "flip" from a legitimate (legal, register and incorporated, and pay your taxes) business compared to the dope game (selling drugs), the returns have a huge difference. For example, a pound of gas, loud, fire, dro, weed [high quality marijuana]) could cost roughly $2,000 depending on your connections (supplier) and location (effects supply and demand). One would resell this product (pound of weed) to a valued customer at $2,500. A $500 profit seems like a lot, especially at one time. Once we break the profit margin down, you had a twenty percent 20% ROI. Most would agree this is a decent flip (profit).

Let's compare a restaurant that sells hamburgers. The cost per unit to make a meal (which includes the materials and food product) is roughly $1.50. An excited hungry customer will purchase this meal at $7.95. After expenditures, this $6.45 profit yields a 530% ROI. We [Black men] have been tricked into thinking the that "street-cents" make more money than the corporate world. We have been taught not to invest in things that do yield a residual return (especially if it positive or legal). As soon as a young black male wants to make some money, why is it that one of the first things to cross his mind is going to the streets and "buying a sac" (buying drugs)? Instant gratification has caused the demise of hard work and thinking a decision all the way through.

We must start thinking outside the cell block and plantation field. We have to practice thinking positive. As black people, we think too deeply about schemes, scams, licks, and quick come-ups. We, as a culture, prefer to have new weave, Jordan's, clothes, and other flashy items, while waiting at the bus stop to be picked up. Many black men and women are wearing a monthly car note, mortgage payment, or an investment into their child's college fund. We have got to do better.

Our black wealth has declined. When we were segregated, Blacks were forced to support businesses in their communities. When blacks integrated, they flocked to support white businesses. Blacks spend 95% of their income at white owned businesses. Unemployment rates for black men increased tremendously; affirmative action has not improved the employment rate for black men. [This system was designed to primarily help white women and some "upwardly mobile black"] (suburbs). Currently, the unemployment rate for black males are 8.4 % compared to white males only being 4.2%.

What did the dope game do for most black men? It gave them leadership and managerial skills that they did acquire because of lack of opportunity. When you walk into a company to get a job, you are not going to receive a job managing money or making business decisions. How and when will they learn? If I were to go look for a job, even having an economics degree, it would be difficult for me to find one. Once I receive the job, the corporate officers would always perceive me as a threat. Now my focus will be job security instead of job performance. The system of white patriarchy is designed to break black men down. How do we build up these broken men, help them attain useful skillsets, plan their businesses, create business plans, and protect their money?

We need to educate and train young black men to be managers and leaders, so they can understand their ability to head households, businesses, and their personal lives. We are not addressing the real issues of my brothers. We have millions of young men with skills, but they lack direction. Most can't go to their fathers because they lack the education or they are not present. We cannot get caught up in the hype of distractions; they are inevitable. One must know how to deal with it and handle it as it comes. As soon as you decided to tackle your business endeavors, you will be distracted. Whatever your vice may be, the distraction will be that and much more. If you appear too successful, someone is going to send their dogs to sniff you out.

Chapter 6: Exposure Affects Composure

What we are exposed to, ultimately dictates how we are composed. Our environments can break and build, hurt and heal, defeat or defy, and ultimately save our lives or cause us to surrender in defeat. Black men have been exposed to overwhelming circumstances for no other reason beyond their unchangeable physical appearances. I am not excusing illegal activities, poor decisions, or lack of education; but I am acknowledging the elephant in the room that our society has dismissively addressed.

Every system in America has strategically disregarded the plight of the black male. One would think the historical election and presidency of President Barack Obama would cause a shift in the burdensome plight of black men. Ironically, it seems that our struggles worsened. Fortunately, I realize that was not the case. However, President Obama posed the greatest threat that America ever experienced. A black man as the most powerful person in the nation. This fact scared the holy-hell out of white patriarchy. Thus, President Obama was met with a resistance from his governmental counterparts that no other president experienced in such a blatant manner – all because he was a black man.

The Presidency of Barack Obama is the most positive exposure many black men accept and respect. The former president's presence in the white house caused black men everywhere to realign their composure socially, politically, personally (family), and professionally. Exposure affects composure. It is impossible to compose yourself in a respectable manner when you constantly experience disrespect and a blatant disregard of your manhood. Fortunately, Black men have never been the type to fold easily under pressure. If we cannot do anything else, we know how to survive and make the best of the most deplorable situations.

Opportunely, circumstances change and opportunities to better ourselves are accessible. We have access to education, financial opportunities, and personal/professional advancement. The more we see, the more we learn. Being exposed to newness opens our mind and allows us to understand and see things from a new perspective.

Exposure is vital because it gives people an opportunity to avoid complacency. Complacency chokes advancement and creates a false sense of satisfaction amid mediocrity. Most people do what they do because they feel as if it's the only way. However, the doors are open, and exit strategies can be implemented to take you from the mediocre to the magnificent. This acceleration towards greatness begins with the way we think.

How are we thinking?

Are the majority thoughts of young blacks full of ignorance, violence, oppression, or self-loathing? Will we use our thoughts to empower each other with wisdom, love, and growth? Are we thinking about longevity for the future, our families, and an inheritance for our children? Or do we simply get caught up in the moment of life and just living? The ideology of "tomorrow is never promised" is an illusion to the thought process. The reality is you might not be here tomorrow, but tomorrow will come (with or without you). Our thought process should be "live in the moment but think for tomorrow."

Chapter 7: Restoring a Positive Personal Image/Identity

There is nothing more influential in our society than the power of the media. The television has always told or proclaimed a vision of what they believe is factual or ideal from products to people. The impact of the media has been astronomically magnified with the onset of social media. Image and identity (of people) are deeply affected by all forms of media. Image is how something looks or might look: the idea that people have about someone or something, or a visual representation of something. Identity is the factual manifestation of who a person is.

The media has created a distorted image of black men that is not a true depiction of our identity. It is not a secret that black men are portrayed in stereotypical negative roles constantly: felons, absent-fathers, unemployed, criminals, misogynistic, uneducated, aggressive, violent, and intimidating. Truth be told, these falsified depictions can only be dismissed by the manifestation of positive images and identities within our society.

We DO NOT have to personify the images that are created by the media as factual!

Reality TV and music depicts black men as wayward/indecisive (especially regarding women/family), money is glorified as the only TRUE love of black men, and they are disconnected from the looming issues our society. However, because the entertainment industry is primarily controlled by white men, these images are perpetuated as truths under the umbrella of "it's just TV, a movie, or social media. It's not real."

On the contrary perception and reality intertwine frequently, and most people perceive the depictions of various ethnic groups as undeniable truths.

Thugs, gangsters, low-life bums, gold teeth, baggie pants. White people don't want to deal with that. Negative depictions and content are the only type of black men white people see and hear about on a regular basis. Repetition is key; the more you see, hear, and look at something, the more believable it is. If you see most of your people on T.V. acting hard and stupid, you will feel compelled to act this way because everybody that looks like you *does* [seemingly].

Why would White America want us to believe we are Thugs?

When black men are born in America, two things are built for them; prison cells and caskets. Thugs are incarcerated and/or killed. In the mind of the white men, we are already perceived as intimidating.

Educated black men are equally intimidating because we are perceived as a threat to the American patriarchal society; unless our intelligence is used for their benefit… then we are considered a *treat*.

What if we made the real black man trendy?

We glorify stupidity. Anything negative is strategically glorified by the media and foolishly perpetuated within our culture. We [Black men] are cool and trending, when we do something, the rest of the world pays attention and follows! So why not do something that is positive? Wear suits and ties, be educated, be empowered, be liberated, be strong, and take a stand for what is right. Let's make being a gentleman the new gangster.

Assimilation.

We don't have to agree with *"their"* agenda. We have freedom and free will. Assimilation is the nemesis of an authentic identity; it requires people to conform and acquire the social and psychological characteristics of a group, specifically the majority.

We see examples of assimilation everywhere because too many people believe it is beneficial. Some will assimilate so much that their characteristics and behavior change. Some people change how they speak, their style of dress, and some go as far as changing their diets. If *some people* could bleach their skin, *they* probably would. The Eurocentric look is glorified by mainstream America and too many blacks conform to this standard of attractiveness or beauty.

Millennials are opposed to this assimilated way of thinking. The younger generation is much more attuned to Afrocentric standards of beauty/attractiveness. We must be who we are designed to be to fulfill our purpose.

Don't get caught up in the wave of what is trending. If the path you need is not there, sometimes you must create your own. We must have pride in ourselves to establish positive legacies. The world will remember us for the marks we make. How do you want to be remembered? Will you assimilate and live their history, or will you create your own? It's time to break out of the shell of insecurities and embrace individuality. Be you and embrace everything about you!

Chapter 8: Accountability versus Responsibility

There is seemingly an epidemic among black men when we consider our level of accountability and responsibility for the state of our families, communities, and ourselves! Fortunately, this problem is easily fixable. Primarily we must understand the obligation of being accountable; accountability is the quality or state of being **accountable or liable**; specifically, an obligation or willingness to account for one's actions and the effect of those actions on others. The circumstances of our lives should not dictate the level of our accountability. We must always consider how our actions will influence the people and things connected to us [it is our responsibility].

This point segues into the importance of black men accepting and upholding our responsibilities. It is always easier to turn a "blind-eye" and ignore problems than it is to approach them head-on and rectify them. Conversely, an ignored problem is still a problem, and more than likely it

35

becomes an extensively magnified problem when it is ignored. Black men our proper place is at the top, we are innate problem-solvers. We cannot continue to allow the things that we should be in control of, to be controlled by others.

Black FAMILIES Matter: The HEAD & Not the Tail!

According to the 2016 U.S. Census, approximately 62% of black children under the age of 18 live in a single-parent household (two-thirds of this group has a female head-of-household). This reality is saddening. It reveals an acceptance of the stereotypical "baby-daddy" and irresponsibility. As men, more than anything else, we should want to oversee our families and ensure their well-being.

Personally, I know too many black men that have two or more "baby-mommas." Black men need to support their children completely, whether they share the same physical address or not. This means, the support of your child cannot be reduced to a mandated deduction from your paycheck –

this is not child support. It is a way to brew animosity and discontentment between you and the mother of your child – while creating a wedge of separation within the black family unit. We must lead by example and think about how our decisions have immediate and latent effects.

I was raised in a two-parent household, and for this I am grateful. I have been able to experience the effect of seeing my father "run the household!" I witnessed him take care of *his* family. He did not scurry away from the responsibility of rearing his family. Rodney Long was accountable for his actions and the effect they had on his family whether they were perceived as "good or bad." Consequently, I cannot say I did not have an example of a strong black man (husband, father, influencer).

Black People & Our Communities

When we enter the black community, we must ask ourselves these questions: Who *controls* our communities? Who *owns* our communities? How are financial resources allocated within our communities? The gas stations and convenience [liquor] stores, are owned by Pacific Islanders. They enter predominantly black communities, put their family members to work, and the revenue from these stores do not benefit our communities in any way. The supermarkets, hardware stores, and most restaurants are owned by other races within our communities. This money is rarely recycled back into black communities; less than 10% of all spending power is used to better our communities.

Consider this factual perspective, black people give away 90% of their power and freedom to other races only to control the growth and direction of their future. The reason nothing changes within our community is because of all the money leaves the community. This lack of financial circulation disallows black business owners to help restore and rebuild our communities.

Financial power resides in the hands of white patriarchy, black people are still at the bottom of the totem pole. Everybody has the power and the ability to have the same greatness even if the same opportunities are not presented [Side note: Black people are the most resourceful people I know. What we do not have, we have the wherewithal to create, [lets tap into that resourcefulness]. No one *should* receive more advantages than someone else because of the color of their skin, but this is an American reality, so we must do what we can to improve our reality!

It is an undeniable FACT that 400 years of slavery contributed to the wealth and income gap in our country among blacks and whites! Black men and women would be financially secure for numerous generations also - if their families attained wealth due to free labor from their "employees" [slaves]!

Chapter 9: Black Men Are We Endangered?

Black Men – "They're putting US on the Endangered Species List!"

THEM: Why are you so angry when cops kill black men, but not when black men kill each other?

Black men glorify killing each other in music and movies.

US: When we kill each other, we don't get away with it. It's the "two birds with one stone" effect; two black men are gone forever. **One black man is dead physically and the other is dead to society because he will spend the rest of his life incarcerated.**

However, between 2005 and April 2017, 80 officers were arrested on murder or manslaughter charges for on-duty shootings of black men in high-profile cases. During this 12-year span, a mere 35% of these police officers were convicted, while the rest are pending or were acquitted, according to work by Philip Stinson, an associate professor of criminal justice at Bowling Green State University in Ohio.

Conversely, someone coined the term "black on black crime" to magnify the occurrence of violent crimes/murder in black communities, while minimizing the murders that occur in white communities [it is not called "white on white crime, and usually it is]. Interesting? Factually, there are more white men that are certified killers; but our society and the media has embedded the face of a black men to be notorious killers and worthy of death because of a presumed threat of danger. This is strategic and unwarranted!

In January of 2016, Republican presidential candidate Jeb Bush in Iowa was asked during a meeting with the editorial page of The Des Moines Register about whether there was a federal role in easing police community relations in the wake of high-profile police shootings. His response was as follows: "Most crimes in *these* communities are "black-on-black," he said. "by far in the predominantly African-

American communities, it's black-on-black crime — the police shooting of unarmed black males, which is what the conversation is about as I understand it, is very small." Bush, is one of many that responds in this manner when the subject of police shootings come up.

We live in a sad state, when black fathers and mothers must discuss "appropriate" ways to interact or behave when and if you are approached by the police with their children. Black children (especially males), are considered a threat. J. Drew Lanham said it best, **"Dead is the new black y'all!"** Race is a lethal condition. Being a man of color, that's the national sin." Men of Color, an endangered species, will the fight for civil equality ever end?

"They" Say We Need an Attitude Adjustment!

Attitude is defined as: the way one thinks and feels about someone or something; a feeling or way of thinking that affects a person's behavior regarding someone or something. So, answer this. How would you think or feel as a black man living in today's societal climate? Are black men angry or comfortable around policemen?

Even when our hands are raised above our heads, [Terence Crutcher] we are shot. When we are walking home, [Trayvon Martin] we are shot. When we are told to show identification, [Philando Castile] we are shot. When we are playing on the playground, [Tamir Rice] we are shot. Being a black makes us target practice for the police, intentionally and systematically. Thus, if an attitude adjustment is needed, it is not the attitude of the black man… but it is attitude of the white man!

From Columbine to the more recent shooting in South Florida, white men kill other white people [heinous crimes, but NOT white on white crime] and they live. Black men are simply trying to live and end up dead. I cannot justify a "Yes Sir," in the face of looming death, but I say it. Could you? I cannot ignore the fear brewing in my stomach, when a police officer pulls me over for "driving while black." I cannot fully explain to my black nieces and nephews why black people are killed by police at a higher rate than any other race, and these police officers are rarely brought to justice.

Finally, I cannot fathom why my attitude should be "adjusted" when I am the one who should be afraid. Fear has awakened the beast in me, and sometimes death is the only way to be truly free. Consequently, I fight for the death of institutional racism, racist stereotypes, racial profiling, so-called "Black on Black Crime," and the inexcusable justification of killing people who look like me too frequently.

Chapter 10: Knowledge Is the Advantage

Education: The process of receiving or giving systematic instruction, typically at a school or university; Or an enlightening experience that produces awareness and understanding of someone or something [example: reading this book].

In education, we lack the proper training for success. Older generations think they are training the youth the right way, but, they are not. I believe black people want the youth to be the leaders of their legacies but *only* on their terms. White families don't create successful businesses just to leave it for their children. While their businesses are thriving and growing, they bring their children into their companies as apprentices and future decision-makers.

The difference between white and black people is that white people take meaningful steps daily to prepare their children and the next generations to take over what they have established. Too many Black people establish businesses in hopes of their children developing the necessary skillset to operate the business. I am certain that Blacks would love to see the next generation excel but many of them are unwilling to give up their authority. Black people fail because we are unprepared. As a people, we are not doing what is takes to prepare *"the future"* for the future.

Our HBCUs [I am a proud alumnus] need to implement strategic and innovative educational models that produce the *best*. If I could enhance anything about our institutions, I would revamp our historic/traditional mentality. HBCU's prepare students to be excellent employees but not employers. We give the credentials to be a professor, but we won't become the vice presidents, program directors, or members of the board of director. We are teaching our students to work for other people. We still have not grasped the concept of *being* the head and not the tail. We are not innovating. New times require new thinking.

We can take the students who are considered "average" and make them entrepreneurs. These will be the students that have experience and opportunities with the local companies in their communities to intern. They will be the students that will be more impactful to their immediate communities. This is creativity and innovation. This would be considered the "white way" of thinking.

The average brother black male who is trying to do something right doesn't ask for help. It's not because they are prideful or stubborn, it is simply because they don't know better. Therefore, we are behind as a culture in American society. The few times when black people eventually ask for help, they only ask people that look like them. We must break this way of thinking and understand that we can never stop learning. Life is a lesson in progress. Every day we learn more about our world, existence, as well as who we are.

The Initiation of Education

What are we teaching our children? They learn from what they see and what they are exposed to. Education starts at home. Black people teach and learn, the question is what are we teaching and what are we learning? Who or what is educating us?

The bulk of our social intelligence is learned from birth to five years old. What are we teaching our babies and what are we exposing them to? Far too many black kids are exposed to twerk videos, "Trap Music," World Star, reality T.V., and drama filled gossip stories. It doesn't make sense for a child to know every word to a song that they hear on the radio, but they cannot recite their alphabet. This is not the child's fault, but it falls solely on the parents. We need to expose our children more to "Leap Frogs," "My Baby Can Read," and other learning programs for children.

Consequently, I asked, "What are the parents doing all day?" How much education or professional training have

48

they acquired? This answer is reflected in their child's behavior and social interactions. Our future will be whatever they are taught *the most*, and we are responsible for this outcome.

Concluding Thoughts

We are responsible for the changes we need and desire. We are accountable for our actions and efforts to make the world we *live* in a better place. I want people to understand the power in understanding the American system of White Patriarchy!

In understanding what works against us, we realize what and who can work for us! If what you're doing is not helping the culture, you're hurting the culture. The truth is this, the world we live in may be controlled by "the white man", but if we understand the tactics used against us, and we can defeat them. I am not telling you to think as if you are the white man. I am simply telling you to attain a comprehensive awareness of what you're up against, so you can be successful

despite the reality of White Patriarchy!

About the Author

Julius M. Long was born and raised in Gainesville, Florida. He received his public education through the School District of Alachua County. Julius completed his undergraduate studies with a concentration in Economics at Florida Agricultural and Mechanical University (FAMU). He is an entrepreneur, political activist, youth advocate, and an audacious renaissance man!

Julius has an innate ability to create opportunity, access and utilize unconventional resources, and strategically maximize his intellectual capabilities for the most lucrative purposes! Although, the reality of his youth and his past were not completely favorable, Julius has not allowed these factors to produce complacency in his life. Fortunately, Mr. Long learned from his mistakes and uses this knowledge to encourage, empower, and educate our upcoming generation.

As an author, he hopes his readers will remain open-minded regarding his insights. Julius believes there is nothing more powerful than a "consciously educated black businessman!" Thus, his first book of this introspective series "Understanding the System of White Patriarchy: Think Like the White Man," provides a raw and intimate dialogue of what it is to be a black man trying to navigate *his* way in a White Patriarchal System.

www.ingramcontent.com/pod-product-compliance
Lightning Source LLC
Chambersburg PA
CBHW071140280326
41935CB00010B/1312